E

DISCARDED

ASIA

• Scarlet Skimmer

Fat-Tailed Scorpion •

Emperor Newt •

AFRICA

INDIAN OCEAN

Bird of Paradise •

• Panther Chameleon

AUSTRALIA

Blue-Ringed Octopus •

WHERE CREATURES
& FOSSILS ARE FOUND

ANTARCTICA

Published in Canada by Tundra Books,
75 Sherbourne Street, Toronto, Ontario M5A 2P9

Published in the United States by Tundra Books of Northern New York,
P.O. Box 1030, Plattsburgh, New York 12901

Library of Congress Control Number: 2007927434

Library and Archives Canada Cataloguing in Publication

Patkau, Karen
    Creatures yesterday and today / Karen Patkau.

ISBN 978-0-88776-833-0

      1. Evolution (Biology) – Juvenile literature.
2. Phylogeny – Juvenile literature. 3. Animals – Juvenile literature. I. Title.

QL49.P383 2008   j591.3'8   C2007-902732-6

We acknowledge the financial support of the Government of Canada through the Book Publishing Industry Development Program (BPIDP) and that of the Government of Ontario through the Ontario Media Development Corporation's Ontario Book Initiative.
We further acknowledge the support of the Canada Council for the Arts and the Ontario Arts Council for our publishing program.

ONTARIO ARTS COUNCIL
CONSEIL DES ARTS DE L'ONTARIO

Medium: Digital

Printed in China

1 2 3 4 5 6   13 12 11 10 09 08

To Michael.

With special thanks to scientists at the Royal Ontario Museum, the Royal Tyrrell Museum, and the Smithsonian; Dr. Jane Berg, Diane Fine, and Ellen Munro.

So many creatures that once existed have disappeared. Their fossils give us clues to how they looked and lived. Scientists discover new fossils all the time and continue to develop new ideas about life on Earth. In this book, descriptions of extinct animals are based on what many scientists today think to be true.

CREATURES YESTERDAY

Diplodocus

I was a giant planting-eating dinosaur, with a big heart and a tiny brain. My neck was so long, I could nibble fern leaves in the forest while standing in an open field.

AND TODAY

Skylark

As I fly, you can hear my warbling song.
Like a theropod of long ago, I have a
wishbone, scaly feet, and hard-shelled
eggs. Am I a living dinosaur?

MOLLUSKS

Cameroceras

I was a huge jet-propelled cone, with eyes, a beak, and many arms. I could squirt a thick black cloud of ink into the waves whenever I needed to escape.

Blue-Ringed Octopus

Find me in a tide pool or a warm shallow reef. I have a soft body and eight arms with suction cups. If my blue rings "glow," back away! My bite can be deadly.

REPTILES

Hylonomus

A pioneer, I climbed out of the lagoon
onto dry land. Being cold-blooded,
I warmed up or cooled off along with
the temperature of the air around me.

Panther Chameleon

I have feet and a prehensile tail, just right for clasping branches. My skin changes color according to the light and what mood I am in. My tongue is lightning-fast.

FISH

Dunkleosteus

A ferocious carnivore, I scoured the ocean for a tasty meal. My jaws were like huge scissors, with sharp jagged edges. Bony armor covered my head and neck.

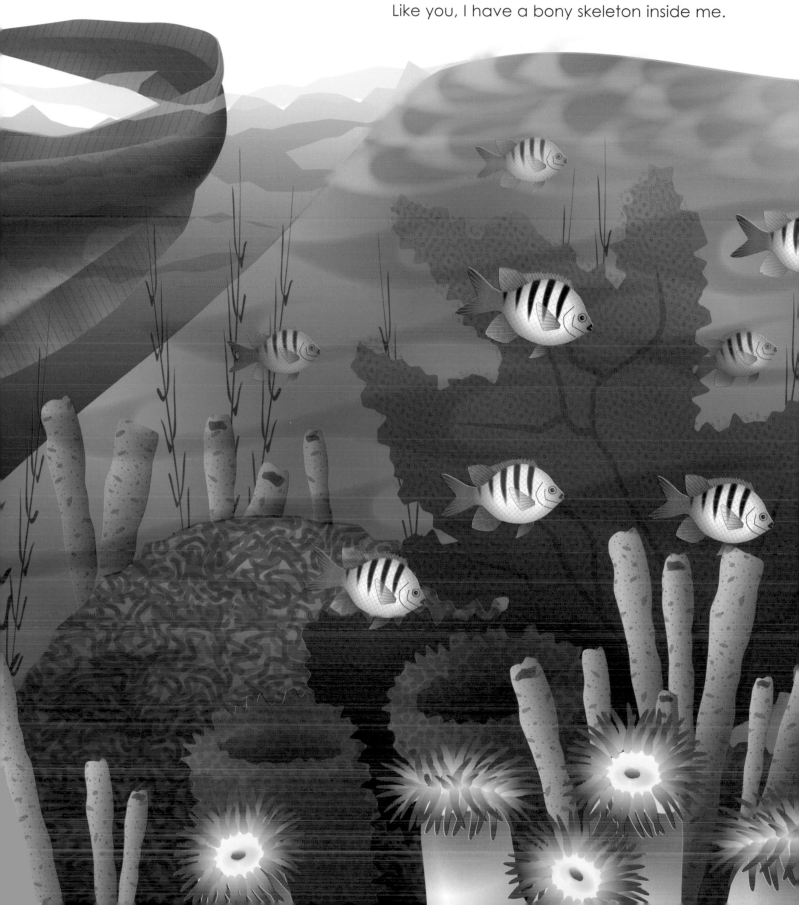

Sergeant Major

Above a bright coral garden, I swim with my school. My air bladder keeps me afloat, while my gills filter oxygen from the water. Like you, I have a bony skeleton inside me.

ARACHNIDS

Brontoscorpio

Look out! I could paralyze you with a sting from my tail, or pinch you with my pedipalps. Breathing through my book lungs, I marched from the floor of the ocean onto the shore.

Fat-Tailed Scorpion

A predator, I rest in my burrow in the daylight. After dark, I venture out into the desert. Comblike sensors on the underside of my exoskeleton tell me where I am.

SEA JELLIES

Rhizostomites

My round squishy body was called a bell. I had stinging cells on "oral arms" around my mouth. I used them for self-defense and to trap a fresh seafood dinner.

Atolla Jelly

So fragile, I may tear apart if you touch me. Through bioluminescence, I light up the briny deep. I move by a pulsing motion, or gracefully float about.

BIRDS

Phorusrhacos

I was called Terror Bird! An awesome, flightless bird of prey, I would charge over vast plains. Could you guess my immense bones were hollow and lightweight?

Bird of Paradise

Perched high in a tree in the rainforest, I do a splendid courtship dance. My noisy squawk is heard from dawn to dusk. I gobble up insects, worms, fruit, and seeds.

AMPHIBIANS

Ichthyostega

An aquatic tetrapod, I paddled in the swamp that cradled my jellylike eggs. Breathing was easy with my nose in the air, but scrambling up a bank was hard.

Emperor Newt

Starting out as a tadpole in a stream, I transform through metamorphosis. My gills turn into lungs. I sprout legs for walking on land. At times, I still like to go for a swim.

MAMMALS

Smilodon

I was a fierce saber-toothed cat, known
for my enormous front fangs. A sly hunter,
I lay in wait in tall grass to ambush quarry.
If you made me angry, I would ROARRR!

Cheetah

My claws grip the ground as I race across
the savanna. I use my long muscular tail
for balance. The fastest runner on Earth, I
dash away. I do not have to stay and fight.

CRUSTACEANS

Canadaspis

I had eyes on stalks and antennae on my head. A bottom-feeder, I used my mandibles to grind my food. With a carapace to protect me, I scuttled over the seabeds.

Antarctic Krill

At night, I surface in icy salt water to feast on phytoplankton. I sink to great depths when I am full. As I grow, I shed my tough outer casing over and over.

INSECTS

Meganeura

I was one of the very first animals to fly and was perhaps the biggest insect ever! Imagine the BUZZZZ my four wings made as I zoomed through the steamy woods.

Scarlet Skimmer

See me dart, dip, and dive in the sunshine.
I am snacking on insects in midair. Below is
the pond where I hatched into a nymph,
before I developed into a dragonfly.

History of Life

Million Years Ago	Periods of Time
543 to today	**PHANEROZOIC EON** • from beginning of Cambrian Period to today
65 to today	**Cenozoic Era** – "recent life" • first modern humans appear in Quaternary Period • first grasses appear in Tertiary Period • many kinds of mammals, including large land and sea animals, evolve
1.8 to today	**Quaternary Period**
65 to 1.8	**Tertiary Period**
248 to 65	**Mesozoic Era** – "middle life" • first flowering plants appear in Cretaceous Period • first birds evolve in Jurassic Period • first dinosaurs and mammals appear in Triassic Period • many of these animals become extinct before end of Mesozoic Era
144 to 65	**Cretaceous Period**
206 to 144	**Jurassic Period**
248 to 206	**Triassic Period**

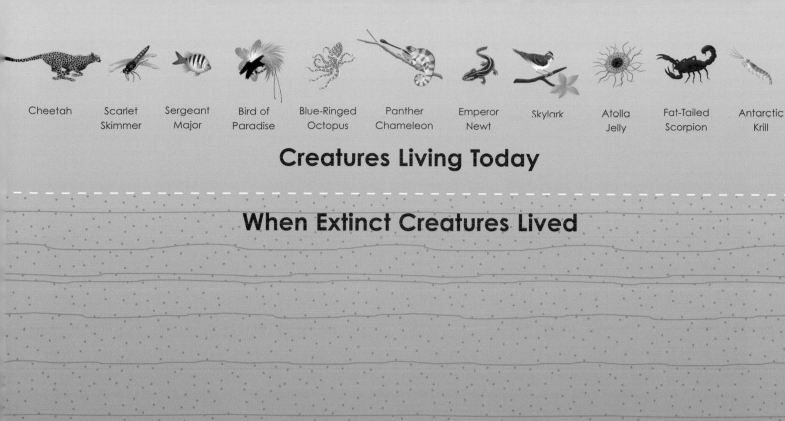

Cheetah   Scarlet Skimmer   Sergeant Major   Bird of Paradise   Blue-Ringed Octopus   Panther Chameleon   Emperor Newt   Skylark   Atolla Jelly   Fat-Tailed Scorpion   Antarctic Krill

Creatures Living Today

When Extinct Creatures Lived

Smilodon / SMY-lo-don

Phorusrhacos / for-us-RAH-kuss

Diplodocus / dip-low-DOCK-us

Rhizostomites / rye-zoh-stoh-MY-teez

Million Years Ago	Periods of Time
543 to 248	**Paleozoic Era** – "ancient life" • complex life-forms appear, including fish, insects, amphibians, reptiles, and land plants • first vertebrates – jawless fish – evolve in Cambrian Period • first vertebrates are our earliest ancestors
290 to 248	**Permian Period**
354 to 290	**Carboniferous Period**
417 to 354	**Devonian Period**
443 to 417	**Silurian Period**
490 to 443	**Ordovician Period**
543 to 490	**Cambrian Period**
4,500 to 543	**PRECAMBRIAN TIME** • 4/5ths of Earth's history • sea life-forms evolve and divide into two main branches – plants and animals • simple life-forms first appear in the seas • Earth's atmosphere forms • Earth's crust forms
4,500	**Earth Forms**

When Extinct Creatures Lived

Meganeura / meg-ah-NEW-rah

Dunkleosteus / dunk-el-AW-stee-us

Hylonomus / hy-low-NO-muss

Ichthyostega / ick-lhee-o-STAY-gah

Brontoscorpio / bron-toe-SCORE-pee-o

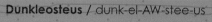

Cameroceras / ka-mare-AW-ser-as

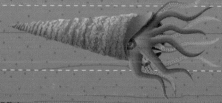

Canadaspis / kan-ah-DASP-is

GLOSSARY

air bladder – an air-filled sac in a fish that controls how it floats underwater

aquatic – developing, growing, or living in water

bioluminescence – a chemical process that produces light within a living thing

book lungs – breathing organs with thin layers of membrane looking like book pages

carapace – a tough case that covers the back of an animal's body

carnivore – a meat-eating animal

evolve – to develop gradually through natural process

exoskeleton – a hard protective covering on the outside of an animal

fossils – remains of ancient animals and plants preserved in rock

lagoon – a shallow body of water that is connected to a larger one

mandibles – mouthparts used for biting and grinding food

metamorphosis – change in the form or structure of an animal as it develops

nymph – early-stage form of some insects

pedipalps – large pincerlike mouthparts used to grab and subdue prey

phytoplankton – very tiny plants that live in water

pioneer – an animal capable of living in a bare or open territory

predator – an animal that hunts other animals for food

prehensile – capable of grasping, especially by wrapping around things

quarry – an animal that is hunted for food

savanna – a flat dry grassland

sensors – feelers that detect such things as movement, texture, light, or heat

tetrapod – an animal with a backbone and four limbs

theropod – a two-legged, meat-eating dinosaur, with sharp teeth and short arms

vertebrates – animals with backbones

NORTH
AMERICA

Ichthyostega

Canadaspsis •

EUR

Brontoscorpio •

Rhizostomi

Diplodocus •

Meganeura •

Cameroceras •

• Dunkleosteu

• Atolla Jelly

PACIFIC OCEAN

C OCEAN

Ch

• Antarctic Krill